The Big Book of Riddles

Lisa Regan

ARCTURUS

ARCTURUS

This edition published in 2019 by Arcturus Publishing Limited
26/27 Bickels Yard, 151–153 Bermondsey Street,
London SE1 3HA

ISBN: 978-1-78404-294-3
CH004219NT

Written by Lisa Regan
Illustrated by Moreno Chiacchiera (Beehive Illustration)
Designed by Notion Design
Edited by Joe Harris, Frances Evans & Joe Fullman

Supplier 26, Date 0319, Print run 8650

Printed in China

Contents

Introduction

On the following pages, you'll find baffling brainteasers, cunning conundrums, and ridiculous riddles that will give your mental muscles a real workout! The solutions can be straightforward or they might require a bit of head scratching. Some will make you laugh, while others are sure to make you groan. Remember, all the answers are in the back, but try not to peek! Right, it's time to get riddling!

Animal
Riddles

1 What single letter can you swap to make a cold bear become hot?

2 You really couldn't carry
The thing that's on my back,
Yours is much too heavy,
But mine will easily crack.
I don't carry any money
Or have your love of wealth,
But I leave silver when I travel,
Moving with such silent stealth.

3 What goes naked to keep you warm?

Answers on page 150

4 What sort of socks do polar bears wear?

5 A polar bear walks 5 km (3 miles) north and then 3 km (2 miles) south. He ends up 8 km (5 miles) from his starting point. How can that be?

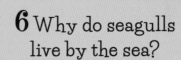

6 Why do seagulls live by the sea?

7 I'm alive without breath
Yet cold as death.
I don't feel thirst but am in the drink.
I'm dressed in chain mail but never clink.

7

Answers on page 150

8 What do giraffes have that no other animal has, which keeps them from going extinct?

9 What is as tall as a giraffe, has a long neck like a giraffe, and four long legs like a giraffe, but doesn't weigh anything at all?

10 Why don't lions eat stand-up comedians?

Answers on page 150

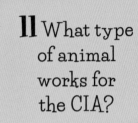

11 What type of animal works for the CIA?

12 I hiss like a frying pan and am made with an egg;
I can move around, though I have no legs.
My skin peels off, but I stay the same.
I'm long and strong - do you know my name?

13 The more you take, the more you leave behind. What are they?

Animal Riddles

9

Answers on page 150

14 Tom has two pet mice, and the number of mice he has doubles every week. In ten weeks, he'll have 1,024 mice. How many weeks before he has over 500 mice? Don't think too hard!

15 There are 25 mice in a school classroom during a class. The mice are moving around, but nobody is looking at them. Why is that?

16 What kind of pet always lives on the floor?

17 What did the mouse say when another mouse broke a tooth?

10

Answers on page 150

18 Why are leopards no good at hiding?

19 Mystery Word

EACH LINE OF THIS PUZZLE IS A CLUE TO A LETTER.
CAN YOU DISCOVER THE HIDDEN WORD?

My first is in wild, and bellow, and water.

My second's in woman and also in daughter.

My third is the very beginning of rough.

My fourth is in bristles in tusks
and in tough.

My fifth is in hairy and cough
but not snout.

You're well on your way to working this out!

My sixth appears twice in the roots
that I munch.

My last is in pig, who's one of my bunch.
What am I?

11

Answers on page 151

20 A frog sits on a lily pad in the middle of a circular pond. He is 12 m (40 ft) from the edge. His first jump takes him to a lily pad 6 m (20 ft) away. After his first jump, he always jumps half the distance of his previous jump. How many jumps must he make to reach dry land?

21 I have a bushy tail but do not sweep,
I stay awake while you're asleep.
Just like a wolf, my fur is brown.
I'm totally wild but live in town.
What am I?

22 How do you describe an exhausted frog?

12

Answers on page 151

23 Joe is taking his dog for a walk. It doesn't walk in front of him, or behind him, or to one side of him. He isn't carrying it, and of course, it isn't above him or below him. Where is his dog?

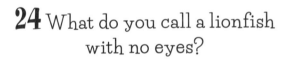

24 What do you call a lionfish with no eyes?

25 This case has no hinges,
No key, no lid,
But golden treasure
Inside is hid.

13

26 A cowboy rides into town on Friday, stays for two days, and leaves on Friday. How can that be?

27 I am a seven-letter word, but if you take away four letters, only one is left. I'm a real beast – you might even say I'm the queen! Who am I?

28 What does a buffalo say to her son when he leaves for school?

14

Answers on page 151

29 A man must cross a river in his rowboat, taking with him a snake, his pet rat, and a sack of grain. The boat is only big enough to carry the man and one item at a time. He can't leave the snake and the rat together, and he can't leave the rat and the grain together. How does he get everything safely across the river?

30 What animal can jump higher than an elephant?

31 What kind of dog has no tail?

15

32 How do you get down from a donkey?

33 What creature walks on four legs in the morning, two legs at noon, and three legs in the evening?

34 What animal wears more in the summer than it does in the winter?

16

Answers on page 152

35 A monkey is tied to the end of a piece of string 1 m (3 ft) long. How did it manage to eat some figs from a bowl 3 m (9 ft) away?

36 A man climbs a ladder and sees an enormous snake. He continues to climb, not scared at all. How can this be?

37 When is a rook not a bird?

17

Answers on page 152

38 When is a swan the same as corn?

39 What has two heads and one tail and walks on four legs?

40 I live in the river but don't have any fins,
If you canoe past, I might tip you in.
When it looks like I'm bored, I'm actually cross.
Even the crocodiles know I'm the boss!

18

Answers on page 152

41 If two birds lay an average of three eggs every day, how many eggs can a peacock lay in three days?

42 Polar bears, penguins, and seals all live in the polar regions. Polar bears hunt seals but never penguins. Why is this?

43 What grows even though it is not alive?

44 What can you find in the middle of Uruguay that can't be found anywhere in Brazil or Bolivia?

Answers on page 152

45 THIS IS A VERY OLD, TRADITIONAL RIDDLE:

As I was going to St. Ives, I met a man with seven wives. Each wife had seven sacks, And every sack had seven cats. Every cat had seven kittens. Kittens, cats, wives, sacks – how many were going to St. Ives?

46 If the alphabet goes from A to Z, what goes from Z to A?

20

Answers on page 152

47 A woman on a safari wanted to take a photo of an elephant with its baby. Why couldn't she?

48 A game reserve boasts in its brochure that it is home to 18 elephants, 200 antelope, and 70 zebras. Unfortunately, a fire destroys the perimeter fence and allows all but six elephants, 58 antelope, and 32 zebras to escape. How many elephants are left for the visitors to see?

49 What lies at a lion's feet without being afraid, keeps up with it even when it runs its fastest, but goes away every night?

21

Answers on page 153

50 A hundred feet in the air, it still has its back on the ground. What is it?

51 Two monkeys sit in each corner of a square cage. They are all looking at each other. How many monkeys can say they are looking at another monkey?

52 How can you drop an egg 3 m (10 ft) without breaking it?

Answers on page 153

53 I have horns but am not an ox. I have only one foot but do not hop. I can travel far without ever leaving home. What am I?

54 Why don't lobsters share?

55 Every morning the farmer had eggs for breakfast. He owned no chickens, and he never got eggs from anyone else's chickens. Where did he get the eggs?

56 What walks all day on its head?

23

Answers on page 153

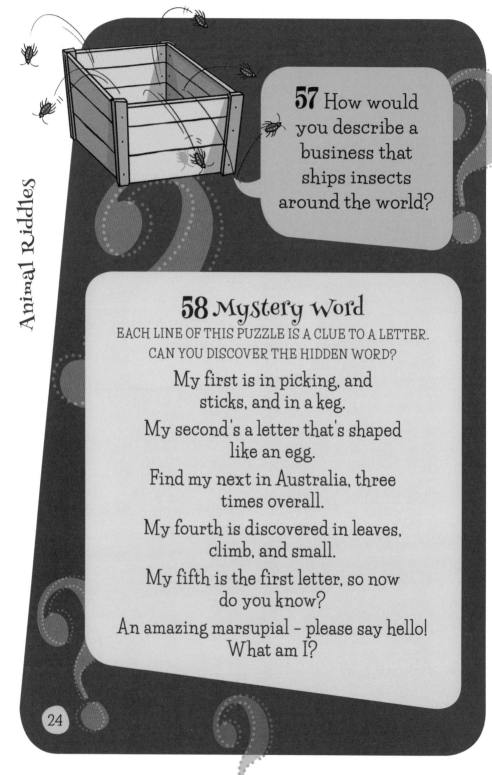

57 How would you describe a business that ships insects around the world?

58 Mystery Word

EACH LINE OF THIS PUZZLE IS A CLUE TO A LETTER. CAN YOU DISCOVER THE HIDDEN WORD?

My first is in picking, and sticks, and in a keg.

My second's a letter that's shaped like an egg.

Find my next in Australia, three times overall.

My fourth is discovered in leaves, climb, and small.

My fifth is the first letter, so now do you know?

An amazing marsupial - please say hello! What am I?

24

59 How many elephants weighing 4,500 kg (5 tons) each can you put in an empty truck that measures 5 m (16 ft) long and 3 m (10 ft) wide?

60 What can you see three times in Madagascar and Antarctica, and twice in New Zealand, but only once in India, France, and Kenya?

61 My feet touch the ceiling, not the floor;
Whatever you hear, I hear much more.
My arms spread wide to give me a boost,
And when daylight comes, I go home to roost.
What am I?

25

62 Mystery Word

EACH LINE OF THIS PUZZLE IS A CLUE TO A LETTER.
CAN YOU DISCOVER THE HIDDEN WORD?

My first begins giant, when I'm fully grown.

My second's in Congo and also in home.

My third is in paper but not ape or man.

My fourth is in rain but isn't in ran.

My fifth is in wobble, and guilty, and flame.

My sixth and my fifth letters both
are the same;

My last is in massive, and awesome,
and great.

The forest and mountains are my
natural state.

What am I?

63 Three-quarters of a lion and
the first half of a donkey;
Join these together for a place
that's really funky.

Answers on page 154

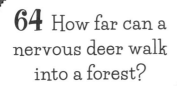

64 How far can a nervous deer walk into a forest?

65 Remove six letters from this word to reveal the name of an endangered animal. PIXAVNTDRAS!

66 1, 2, 3, 4, 5,
These days you won't find me alive.
6, 7, 8, 9, 10,
I'm a 'terrible lizard' from way back when.

67 Why did the man go into the forest without any clothes on?

27

Answers on page 154

Say these tongue-twisters as fast as you can without making a mistake!

The big bug bit the little beetle, but the little beetle bit the big bug back.

My walking stick stinks.
My walking stick is an extinct insect.

A skunk sat on a stump and thought it stunk. Which stunk, the stump or the skunk?

Around the Home

1 If a red house is made of red bricks and a brown house is made of brown bricks, what is a green house made of?

2 What goes up and down the stairs without moving?

3 I turn around once,
What is out will not get in.
I turn around again,
What is in will not get out.
What am I?

Answers on page 154

4 What comes with a car, goes with a car, is of no use to the car, but the car cannot go without it?

5 There are two in a corner, but only one in a room; there is one in an apartment and one in a shelter, but none in a mansion. What is it?

6 What mode of transport has eight wheels but can only carry one passenger?

7 What has six wheels and flies?

Answers on page 154

8 I ask no questions but you feel the need to answer me. What am I?

9 I sing when I'm struck or whenever they shake me. By careful casting, the craftsmen make me.

10 What do you break just by saying its name?

11 What do you call a man who stands outside the front door all day?

Answers on page 154

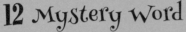

12 Mystery Word

EACH LINE OF THIS PUZZLE IS A
CLUE TO A LETTER. CAN YOU DISCOVER
THE HIDDEN WORD?

My first is in bread, but
never in dear,
My second's in yell, and
also in cheer.
My third is in duffle and also in hood,
My fourth is in word but isn't in wood.
My fifth and my sixth are letters the same
A baboon and a rooster have two
in their name.
My last is in temper, and moody, and slam.
My whole is at home - do you know
where I am?

13 What advice do you get from your hands?

33

14 What belongs to you, but other people use it much more than you do?

15 You have to poke me in the eye to get me to do what you want. I often live in a box but you'd never find me in a haystack. What am I?

16 Toby's mother went into hospital to have her appendix removed. His sister went into hospital a month later to have her tonsils taken out. A week after that, Toby needed a growth from his head removed. Why didn't he go to hospital too?

34

Answers on page 155

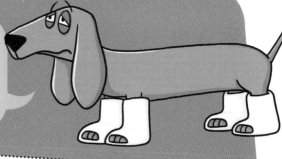

17 What has four legs and a back, but can't walk?

18 I am buried in wood from one end to the other, but my head is on show while I hold things together. Do you know what I am?

19 Divided, we are four families - two are red and two are black. What are we when we are together?

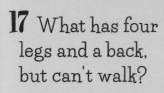

20 I am very good at what I do,
I do my job whenever
you want,
And I'm always on time...
But nobody likes me.
What am I?

Answers on page 155

21 What is two feet long but can be all different sizes?

22 What is being described here?
When I am full I can point the way,
But when I am empty I lie still.
I keep you warm on a snowy day,
But I'm useless when it's sunny.

23 Why did the computer nerd throw away his shirt?

24 What has a neck but no head, and two arms but no hands?

Answers on page 155

25 What happened to the shopper who confused the cobbler's with the baker's?

26 I have a tongue but no mouth. I am no good to you on my own. What am I?

27 When is a coat no use to keep out the cold?

28 What is shown here?
Wear
Clean

37

29 What five-letter word becomes shorter when you add two letters to it?

30 A tablet and a cry of pain – put them together and you can rest your sore head. What am I?

31 What has a head and a tail, but no legs?

32 Rosie's mother has three daughters. She has chosen their names very carefully. The oldest is called April and the middle one is called May. What is the youngest one called?

Answers on page 155

33 Mystery Word

EACH LINE OF THIS PUZZLE IS A CLUE TO A LETTER.
CAN YOU DISCOVER THE HIDDEN WORD?

My first is in large and also in big,
My second's in wait but isn't in twig.
My third is in car, and in ride, and
in truck,
My fourth is in sat but isn't in stuck.
My fifth is in gas but isn't in tanks,
My sixth is in creaks but isn't
in cranks.
Work out the letters and write each
one down;
My whole can be found by a
house or in town.

34 Which burns longer, a short fat candle or a tall thin one?

39

35 Sally throws a ball as hard as she can, but it comes straight back to her without bouncing off anything. How did she do it?

36 What is served but never eaten?

37 There are eight of us
To move at will,
We protect our king
From any ill.
What are we?

40

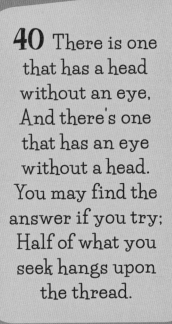

38 What do a zip, a comb, and a shark all have in common?

39 What is as round as a frying pan and as deep as a sink, yet all the oceans in the world couldn't fill it up?

40 There is one that has a head without an eye, And there's one that has an eye without a head. You may find the answer if you try; Half of what you seek hangs upon the thread.

41

Answers on page 156

41 A mother has two sons who share a birthday and were born in the same year – but they are not twins. How could this happen?

42 How can you tell that birthdays are good for you?

43 What has a face and two hands but no arms or legs?

44 What time of day is the same spelled either way round?

Answers on page 156

45 Dita has bought presents for her two sisters. Both presents do the same thing. One has many moving parts, but the other has none. One works all the time, but the other doesn't work at night. What did she buy?

46 What word begins and ends with an 'e' but has only one letter in it?

47 What stays in the corner but travels around the world?

48 Which month has 28 days?

49 If you screw a light bulb into a socket by turning the bulb clockwise with your right hand, which way would you turn the socket with your left hand in order to unscrew it while holding the bulb still?

50 What has rivers but no water, cities but no people, and forests but no trees?

51 What do extra-terrestrial cats drink their milk from?

52 What is always hot, even if you keep it in the fridge?

44

Answers on page 157

53 Please don't drop me or I will crack.
Give me a smile and I'll always smile back.
What am I?

54 What gets wetter the more it dries?

55 What is full of holes, but holds water?

56 What can you find in the bathroom, in music, and on a snake?

Answers on page 157

57 Tom and Harry are sitting on opposite sides of the kitchen table. The table is the only thing between them, their eyes are open and the lights are on - so why can't they see each other?

58 You have a bag with four apples in it. You want to give an apple each to your mother, father, brother, and sister. How can you do that and still have an apple left in the bag?

59 When can you add 2 to 11 to get 1? (No fractions or negative numbers needed!)

46

60 Jill and her friend Jack always wind each other up. This time, Jill says to Jack, 'If you sit on that chair, I bet I can make you stand up before I have run around the chair three times.' Jack knows what Jill is like, and makes her promise not to tickle him or even touch him. 'I promise,' says Jill. 'When you get out of the chair, it will be totally your own choice.' Jack accepts the challenge, but Jill wins the bet. How does she do it?

61 Fill me with air and I fly,
But fill me too much and I die.
What am I?

47

62 Chris goes to the shop to buy something for his house. One would cost him 1.50 and two would cost the same, but 12 would cost him 3 and 122 would cost him 4.50. What is he buying?

63 I can be 'cracked', I can be 'played', I can be 'taken', I can be 'made'. What am I?

64 Poke your fingers in my eyes and I will open my jaws for you. Cloth, leather, cardboard, or paper, I greedily devour them all.

48

Answers on page 158

65 I have space but no room, and keys but no locks. I can return without leaving. I can shift without moving. I never speak but there's no word I cannot make. What am I?

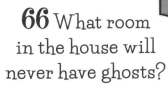

66 What room in the house will never have ghosts?

67 What brings things to life, is never alive, but can still die?

68 What has a spine but no bones, and leaves but no seeds?

49

Answers on page 158

69 Mystery Word

EACH LINE OF THIS PUZZLE IS A CLUE TO A LETTER.
CAN YOU DISCOVER THE HIDDEN WORD?

My first is in kitchen and
counter and hot,
My second's in zero and also not.
My next is in baking and bread and
in taste,
My fourth is in cooks and also
in waste.
For my fifth, you write down my first
once again,
For my sixth, find a letter in duke and
in reign.
My last is in cherry but never
in cheesy,
My whole helps you cook
something yummy but easy.

70 When is a door
not a door?

50

Answers on page 158

71 Three brothers share a family sport:
A non-stop marathon.
The oldest one is fat and short
And trudges slowly on.
The middle brother's tall and slim
And keeps a steady pace.
The youngest runs just like the wind,
Speeding through the race.
'He's young in years, we let him run,'
The other brothers say,
'Cause though he's surely number one,
He's second, in a way.' Why is that?

72 Can you name ten body parts
that are spelt with three letters?

Answers on page 158

Try these tongue twisters:

Which wristwatches are Swiss wristwatches?

Good blood, bad blood.

Flash message! Flash message!

Whether the weather be cold, or whether the weather be hot,
Whether the weather be warm, or whether the weather be not...
We'll weather the weather, whatever the weather,
Whether we like it or not!

Down on the
Farm

1 True or false? There are only two 'F's in 'Farmer Fuffle'.

2 What is all ears and says 'shhhh', but doesn't listen to a word you say?

3 A tree grows an average of 10 branches for each 1 m (3 ft) of height. An average branch grows 12 nuts. How many acorns would a farmer find on a chestnut tree that is 9 m (30 ft) tall?

54

4 Which is the correct: The yolk of the egg is white, or the yolk of the egg are white?

5 Farmer Bob was asked how many eggs he had sold in one day. He replied, 'My first customer said, 'I'll buy half your eggs and half an egg more.' My second and third said the same thing. When I had filled all three orders, I sold out of eggs without having to break a single egg.' How many eggs did he sell?

6 When is the best time to buy chicks?

Answers on page 159

7 What gets bigger, the more you take away from it?

8 In the warm months, I wear green, both during the day and at night. As it cools, I wear yellow, but during winter, I wear white. What am I?

9 The grand old nag gallops with great delight,
Then it grazes on grass and sleeps at night.
A good, strong friend for the farmer and me,
Now – how many times did you count 'g'?

Answers on page 159

10 Mystery Word

EACH LINE OF THIS PUZZLE IS A CLUE TO A
LETTER. CAN YOU DISCOVER THE HIDDEN WORD?

My first is in chew and also in cud,
My second's in goad but isn't in
good.
My third and my fourth are
letters the same,
Found in cart and in tractor,
in stock and in train.
My fifth is in lamb and in billy
but not beef.
My last is in sleep and rest and relief.
My whole can be found on a farm,
big or small.
Even when you can't see me, you'll
still know my call.

11 Where does the biggest herd of pigs live?

Answers on page 159

12 What has eight legs and flies?

13 I'm white and round, but I'm not always around. When the day is at its brightest, I cannot be found. What am I?

14 Farmer Sally builds three haystacks in her north field and two in her south field. Every week afterward, for five weeks, she doubles the number in the north field and adds two more in the south field. How many bales of hay will she have at the end of the harvest if she puts them all together?

Answers on page 16●

15 Farmer Jennings was in town for the day. He went down Main Street without stopping at the red lights and turned into a street that said 'NO ENTRY.' A policeman waved as he went past and didn't give him a ticket or even tell him off. Why was that?

16 When is a black dog not a black dog?

17 What do you call an experienced vet?

59

Answers on page 160

Whatever the weather:

18 What's written here?
BOLT
TH

19 Flowers grow up in the warmth of summer. This grows down in the cold of winter. What is it?

20 You can feel it, but you can't touch it. You can hear it, but you can't see it. What is it?

Answers on page 160

21 What flies when it is born, lies around during its lifetime, and runs when it is dead?

22 Red, purple, orange, Yellow, blue, and green. No one can touch me, Not even a queen. What am I?

23 Daisy wakes up one morning and, without getting up or opening her eyes, knows that it has been snowing. How is this possible?

61

24 What do you find in a hurricane, on a potato, and on the farmer that grows the second and sees the first coming?

25 A farmer was hard at work building a fence when a tiny thing stopped her. Although she didn't want it, she kept on looking for it. Eventually, she took it home with her because she couldn't find it. What was it?

26 What does a dog do that a person steps into?

Answers on page 160

27 Mystery Word

EACH LINE OF THIS PUZZLE IS A CLUE TO A LETTER.
CAN YOU DISCOVER THE HIDDEN WORD?

My first is in goats and also in sheep,
My second's in paw but isn't in weep.
My third is in wood but isn't in grow,
My fourth's just the same as my third,
don't you know.
My fifth is in bleated and cluck
and in squealed,
My sixth is in stable and meadow
and field.
My whole is an item you need for a horse,
Though the horse is quite happy without
one, of course!

28 Read this riddle to a friend out loud:
'There are 20 sick sheep in a field, and
six of them have
to be taken to
the vet. How
many are left?'

63

29 Picture a bridge 4 km (2.5 miles) long and strong enough to hold exactly 9,980 kg (22,000 pounds), but no more. A loaded truck weighing exactly 9,980 kg drives onto the bridge. At the mid point, a sparrow weighing 30 grams (1 ounce) lands on the truck, yet the bridge doesn't collapse. How could this be?

30 How did the farmer find his lost daughter?

31 Most animals grow up. Which animals grow down?

64

32 Every dawn begins with me,
At dusk, I'm the first thing you see,
And daybreak couldn't start without
What midday's middle is all about.
All through the night, I won't be found,
Yet in the dark, I'm still around.
What am I?

33 Forward I am heavy, but backward I am not. What am I?

34 How would you describe a man who does not have all his fingers on his left hand?

Answers on page 161

35 Farmer Jones gets home after a long day harvesting. It is dark, and he is cold and hungry. He has a candle, a stove, and a fireplace but only a single match. Which should he light first?

36 I fly through the air with the greatest of ease. And I am also something you do to your peas.

37 The farmer was worried that her prize currant bush would never grow back after a cold winter. What did she say when she saw it was healthy and green?

Answers on page 161

38 How many bricks does it take to complete a brick barn, measuring 9 m (30 ft) by 9 m (30 ft) by 12 m (40 ft) and made completely of bricks?

39 I have six legs, four eyes, and five ears. What am I?

40 What always runs but never walks, Often murmurs but never talks. Has a bed but never sleeps, Has a mouth but never eats?

Answers on page 161

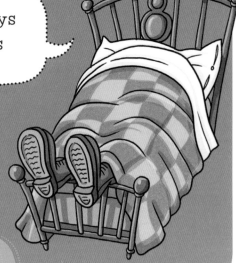

41 Farmer Jake was on one side of the river, and his trusty dog, Elmer, was on the other side. There was no bridge or boat. The farmer whistled to Elmer and shouted, 'Here boy! Come on!' Elmer crossed the river, and they both walked back to the farmhouse. However, Elmer didn't get wet – how can that be?

42 What always sleeps with its shoes on?

43 What goes up and down but doesn't move?

Answers on page 161

44 Mystery Word

EACH LINE OF THIS PUZZLE IS A CLUE TO A LETTER.
CAN YOU DISCOVER THE HIDDEN WORD?

My first is in prarie and turnip
and spade,
My second's in blood but isn't in blade.
My third is in vegetable and also in fruit,
My fourth is in boat but never in boot.
Now write down my third again,
easy as pie,
Then end with my second, and
let out a sigh.
I have skin, I have eyes, but still
I am blind.
Can you figure out my
name from the letters
you find?

45 When is a
tractor not
a tractor?

69

Answers on page 161

46 If a farmer sees 13 crows at the edge of his cornfield and shoots one, how many crows will be left?

47 I have four sails, but I am no boat. I make a meal of wheat or oats. On the same spot, I'm always found, Turning around with a creaking sound.

48 Why did the farmer stand behind the angry horse?

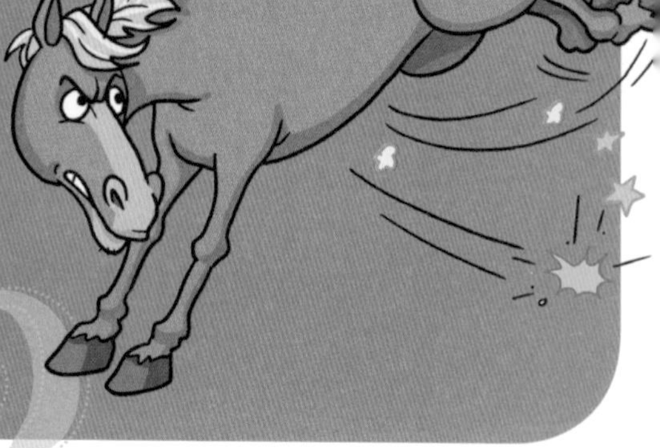

70

Answers on page 161

49 The more you have of it, the less you see. A box is full of it until you open the lid. What is it?

50 Farmer McGinty and his wife walk into the cowshed. They have four cows sheltering there. All of a sudden, they hear meowing and barking, and in rushes the farm cat, Tigger. He is being chased by their dog, Buster, who screeches to a halt by Farmer McGinty. Buster barks at Tigger, who has leaped into Mrs. McGinty's arms. How many feet are there in the barn?

51 What do you call a group of cattle who like jokes?

71

Answers on page 162

52 Farmer Molly went to market. She was selling her beautiful pies. If she sold half of them, plus half a pie, and she had two whole pies left, how many pies had she taken to market?

53 I have a little house where I live all alone. It has no doors and no windows, and if I want to go out, I must break through the wall. What am I?

54 What animal sound goes around and around a tree?

Answers on page 162

55 What four letters did the farmer shout at the apple thieves to frighten them away?

56 What do you call a cow that gives no milk?

57 What kind of horse has no legs?

58 Billy and Jack sneaked into the farm shop to eat their their mother's fudge. Billy's face ended up covered in fudge, but Jack's face was clean. Why did Jack run away to wash his face when he heard his mother approaching, while Billy stayed where he was?

Answers on page 162

59 A farmer raises barley in the dry season and goats all year round. What does he raise in the wet season?

60 Mystery Word

EACH LINE OF THIS PUZZLE IS A CLUE TO A LETTER.
CAN YOU DISCOVER THE HIDDEN WORD?

My first is in middle but isn't in mile,
My second's in oil but isn't in dial.
My third is in animal and barn
and in fence,
My fourth is in nickel but not note,
coin, or pence.
My fifth is in hear and in taste
and in see,
My last is in thirty but isn't in three.
My whole is an animal that's gentle
and kind;
Pet me and stroke me – I really
won't mind.

Answers on page 162

61 A worm is at the bottom of a 101-cm (40-inch) hole. It crawls up at a rate of 10 cm (4 inches) in one day, but at night, it slips back 7.5 cm (3 inches). At this rate, how long will it take the worm to crawl out of the hole?

62 What breaks but never falls, and what falls but never breaks?

63 What's more dangerous than being with a fool?

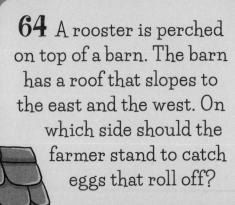

64 A rooster is perched on top of a barn. The barn has a roof that slopes to the east and the west. On which side should the farmer stand to catch eggs that roll off?

75

Answers on page 163

See how fast you can say these tongue twisters

Mares eat oats and does eat oats.

A tricky, frisky snake with sixty superscaly stripes.

Farmer Freddy found the ferret in the farmhouse.

Mealtime Mysteries

1 Is it possible to drop an unboiled egg onto a concrete kitchen floor without cracking it?

2 What two things can you eat but never have for lunch?

3 I am a food
With three letters in my name.
Lose the last two,
And I still sound the same.

Answers on page 163

4 Which fast food gets hotter when it sounds colder?

5 Here's a rhyme to test your head;
We'll call it the tale of Ruby Red.
A stick in her top,
A pit in her middle,
I'll give you a prize
If you answer this riddle.

6 How many peas are there in a pod? Say it out loud!

79

Answers on page 163

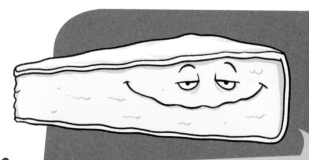

7 I have some cheese.
He has some cheese, too.
And so does she.
They are all the same type of cheese.
What type is that?

8 Let us find the hidden vegetable.
Speak aloud to figure it out.
When we've found the
hidden vegetable,
Let us give a happy shout.

9 What type of
cheese is made
backward?

Answers on page 164

10 Mystery Word

EACH LINE OF THIS PUZZLE IS A CLUE TO A LETTER.
CAN YOU DISCOVER THE HIDDEN WORD?

My first is in pasta and soup and in pit,
My second's in biscuit, in whisk,
and in whip.
My third is in ice cream, chocolate
chip, and cake,
My fourth is in cooking and also in
bake.
My fifth is in apple but isn't in pear,
My last is in fare but isn't in flair.
Put all the letters together to spell
Something that goes with cheese
really well.

11 Which fruit's name describes it?

12 Why do snails never go to hamburger joints?

Answers on page 164

13 What begins with T, ends with T, and has T in the middle?

14 Cows drink it and most people have some in their coffee. What am I thinking of?

15 What cup can't you drink from?

16 What has a neck and a bottom but no head?

Answers on page 164

17 What will you find in the middle of a pie that isn't used in a cake, turnover, or tart?

18 A braggart likes to boast,
And a boat sails
off from the coast.
But what do you put
in a toaster?

19 What kind of
nut has a hole?

83

Answers on page 164

20 What letter tastes of chocolate?

21 Katie's mother went shopping for Katie's birthday party. She bought six pizzas, three cucumbers, twelve carrots, six cartons of strawberries, and forty cupcakes. Katie's brother and his friends raided the refrigerator and ate all but two cucumbers, eight carrots, a carton of strawberries, and seven cupcakes. How many carrots were left?

22 What am I?
Tree ... growth ... red.
Me ... mouth ... fed!

Answers on page 164

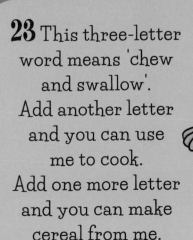

23 This three-letter word means 'chew and swallow'. Add another letter and you can use me to cook. Add one more letter and you can make cereal from me.

24 What has to be broken before it is useful?

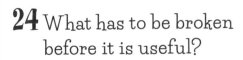

25 I wear a crown, but I'm not a king. I have scales, but I'm not a snake. On the outside, I'm tough, but on the inside, I'm sweet. What am I?

85

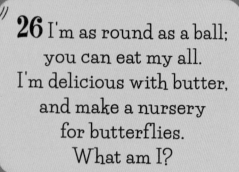

26 I'm as round as a ball;
you can eat my all.
I'm delicious with butter,
and make a nursery
for butterflies.
What am I?

27 What food is written here?
POTOOOOOOOO

28 I make people whine, but they
like me a whole bunch. What am I?

29 I have the same
number of oranges as
my friend. How many
would I have to give
her so that she has 10
more oranges than
I have?

86

Answers on page 165

30 Mystery Word

EACH LINE OF THIS PUZZLE IS A CLUE TO A LETTER.
CAN YOU DISCOVER THE HIDDEN WORD?

My first is in tasty and also in squish,
My second's in ship but isn't in fish.
My third is in pudding and also in rice,
My fourth is in nasty but also in nice.
My fifth is the first of the vowels,
it's true.
My sixth is in crunch and in lick
and in chew.
My last is in dish but isn't in side,
I am really healthy - you'll eat
me with pride!

31 What kind of shoe would be a disaster on Pancake Tuesday?

32 What food has six letters, but if you chop away half of it, you are left only with the item to cook it in?

87

33 If your mother carries three bags of groceries into the house, and she makes you carry six bags, who has the heaviest load?

34 What food starts off hard but gets softer and goes bang as it changes?

35 Go on red and stop on green. Your teeth will know just what I mean. What am I?

88

Answers on page 165

36 I wear a cap but have no head;
Pick the wrong one and you might be dead.
I stand up straight but have no feet;
Pick the right one and I'm good to eat.

37 Which of these is the odd one out? Banana, orange, egg, pistachio, apple, avocado.

38 Time for some arithmetic! If it takes four minutes to boil an egg, how long will it take to boil 367 eggs?

89

39 Two fathers and two sons are at the supermarket. They want a pizza each, and the store has plenty, but they only buy three. Why is that?

40 I have eyes but cannot see. My jacket is brown, but I don't wear clothes. My skin can be red, white, or brown, but I never need sunscreen. What am I?

Answers on page 166

41 What food sounds like a frightened person?

42 A man in a cafe orders a lunch of soup, apple pie, and a black coffee. How does the waitress know he's a policeman?

43 You throw away the outside and cook the inside. Then you eat the outside and throw away the inside. What is it?

44 What is black when you buy it, red when you're making dinner, and silvery when you throw it away?

Answers on page 166

45 If an ice cream sundae with sauce costs 2.10, and the sundae costs 2.00 more than the sauce, how much does a sundae without sauce cost?

46 You'll find me most in sunny lands, I have palms, but I don't have hands. They call me nuts, but that's not true, Both milk and food I give to you.

47 HOW MANY TIMES DOES THE LETTER 'F' APPEAR IN THIS SENTENCE? 'Friends will not feel full of food after eating if they feel that your food is merely a trifle!'

92

Answers on page 166

48 Toby's mother works at the local delicatessen. She tries to be good, but she often eats olives and salami between meals. She is 1.67 m (5 ft 6 inches) tall and a size 12. Toby is 1.55 m (5 ft 1 inch) tall and an average weight for a 12-year-old boy. What does Toby's mother weigh?

49 Which three-letter food can be added to these words to make new words?

Head, cup, shell.

50 There are two types of fruit in the fruit bowl. If you rearrange the letters of one, you get the other. What are they?

93

51 Why do Chinese people eat more rice than French people?

52 How can you spell 'candy' in two letters?

53 At first, you'll find me in the ground.
I'm round and brown and make no sound.
You peel me and cut me, but my oh my -
I get my revenge by making you cry.

54 What comes next?
'Time flies like
an arrow.
Fruit flies like ...'

Answers on page 166

55 On a plate are some vanilla, chocolate, and strawberry cupcakes. All except four taste of vanilla, and all except four taste of strawberry. How many cupcakes are there?

56 Mystery Word

EACH LINE OF THIS PUZZLE IS A CLUE TO A LETTER. CAN YOU DISCOVER THE HIDDEN WORD?

My first is in pod and also in peas,
My second's in cracker and butter
and cheese.
My third and my fourth are the same
as each other,
They're in pop and in parent but never
in brother.
My fifth is in bear but isn't in bar,
My sixth is in pitcher and also in jar.
My whole's used in cooking, as much
as you please,
When you find me, be careful – I may
make you sneeze.

Answers on page 167

57 Dad is going to go BALLISTIC! I was trying to help by washing the dishes ... but I've flooded the kitchen. I left the water running while I watched TV! When I finally remembered, the sink was overflowing, and the floor was like a wading pool. There are dry cloths in the closet, a mop by the door, and a new pack of sponges on the shelf, but I don't know what to do first! What should I do?

58 Look at these glasses. You are allowed to move only ONE glass. How can you arrange them so that the empty and full glasses alternate?

Answers on page 167

59 What weighs nothing, but if you put it in a barrel of water, it will make the barrel lighter?

60 I am as squishy as a banana
But eaten as a vegetable.
I have a tough skin and a hard heart,
But I'm soft in the middle.
I'm slimy and green and grow very high,
But I'm bursting with goodness if you give me a try!

61 Marie has twenty guests at her party. They all stand around the room so that every person can see every other guest without moving. Where can Marie's mother put a cupcake so that everyone in the room can see it, except Marie?

97

62 Mystery Word

EACH LINE OF THIS PUZZLE IS A CLUE TO A LETTER.
CAN YOU DISCOVER THE HIDDEN WORD?

My first is in sandwich and waffle and stew,
My second's in age but isn't in grew.
My third is in garlic and lettuce and kale,
My fourth is in nibble, in snack, and in snail.
My fifth is in pudding and custard,
and yummy,
My sixth begins treat - so nice in
your tummy!
My whole is a food that is so good for you,
Now see if you like me - hurray if you do!

63 What vegetable is only
ever sold fresh - never canned,
pickled, dried, or frozen?

64 If there are three
bananas and you take
away two, how many
bananas do you have?

Answers on page 167

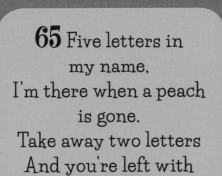

65 Five letters in
my name,
I'm there when a peach
is gone.
Take away two letters
And you're left with
only one.

66 I have five letters and can be
described in four words: sow, grow,
mow, dough. What food am I?

67 If you hold five
apples in one hand
and four apples
in the other hand,
what do you have?

99

Answers on page 167

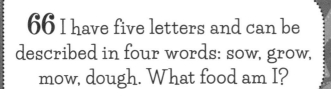

Get your mouth around these tongue-twisters if you can!

Peter Piper picked a peck of pickled peppers. A peck of pickled peppers Peter Piper picked.
If Peter Piper picked a peck of pickled peppers, where's the peck of pickled peppers Peter Piper picked?

I'd like a proper cup of coffee from a proper copper coffee pot.

Mix a box o' mixed biscuits with a boxed biscuit mixer.

Betty Botter bought some bitter butter, but a bit of better butter made her bitter butter better.

Riddles
at
School

5x6x?=

1 Charlie's mother has just gone into his bedroom to wake him for school. She asked him a question, and she knows for sure that he lied when he answered. How can she be so certain?

2 In an arithmetic class, the teacher asks: 'How may seconds are there in a year?' Amresh says, 'Twelve.' The teacher thinks for a moment, then says, 'Yes, that's correct.' How can that be?

3 What does this say?
YYUR
YYUB
ICUR
YY4 me!

Answers on page 168

4 The school librarian sets her class a challenge. 'Let's say there is a banknote hidden in this library. If any of you can find it, then you may keep it as a prize. The money is slotted between pages 57 and 58 of a nonfiction title.' Half of the class jump up and start pulling books off the shelves, The other half don't even leave their chairs. Why not?

5 Brutus the dog was born in 5 BC and died exactly ten years later. In what year did he die?

6 Which word has the most letters in it?

Answers on page 168

7 Some kids are playing hide-and-seek. One of them is the seeker. What is the smallest number of children hiding if:
a girl is hiding to the left of a boy;
a boy is hiding to the left of a boy;
two boys are hiding to the right of a girl.

8 How many times does the letter 'o' appear in the following sentence? 'Boys often play football at school, and girls often choose to play hockey.'

9 What am I thinking of? I can take away the whole, and still have some left.

Answers on page 168

10 Mystery Word

EACH LINE OF THIS PUZZLE IS A CLUE TO A DIFFERENT
LETTER. CAN YOU DISCOVER THE HIDDEN WORD?

My first begins speech but also ends books,

My second is in sees but never in looks.

My third is in nice and also in not,

My fourth is a drink you can make in a pot.

My fifth is the same as my second -
that's handy!

My sixth's in vanilla and bonbon and candy.

My seventh appears in country,
scene, and place,

My eighth's at the end of the tale and the race.

My whole can be written or spoken by any,

But my beginning and end are
forgotten by many.

What am I?

Riddles at School

11 What do pixies
learn first at school?

105

Answers on page 168

12 A triangle has three sides and a square has four. Why might you say that a bubble has two?

13 If you multiply two by itself twenty times, what answer will you get?

14 Mathematics teacher Mrs David asked Alex to multiply five numbers together. She read out each, one at a time, but after just one number, he knew the answer. How could that be?

5×6×?=

Answers on page 169

15 Can you find a way to make 1,000 with eight '8's and four plus signs?

16 What number, when written as a word, has its letters in alphabetical order? (For example, it isn't two, since the 'o' comes before 't' and 'w' in the alphabet.)

17 What is this?
A kind of learning you just don't get at school,
Teachers love it, but pupils think it's cruel,
Your parents might help if they are cool!

107

18 A history teacher shows the class two coins. One is a silver coin with the date 368 BC, and the other is a bronze coin dated AD 798. Which one is worth the most?

19 Why couldn't a centurion living in Roman Britain be legally buried in France?

20 How many ancient philosophers were born in Greece?

Answers on page 169

21 What kind of ship would it take to forge an alliance between enemy pirates?

22 No matter how many shields and helmets I smash, you will still own something mightier than me. What am I?

23 What flies through the air using borrowed feathers?

24 Halo of water, Tongue of wood. Skin of stone, For ages I've stood. What am I?

109

25 Recipe:
Take one season.
Add seasoning.
Roll it over and over.
What do you get?

26 I make my mark
On book or card,
But I will break
If you press too hard.

27 What has hands but no
fingers, a face but no eyes,
and moves all the time
without leaving the spot?

110

Answers on page 169

28 Two's company and three's a crowd, so what do four and five make?

29 Mystery Word

EACH LINE OF THIS PUZZLE IS A CLUE TO A DIFFERENT LETTER. CAN YOU DISCOVER THE HIDDEN WORD?

My first is in add but not in subtract,

My second is in picked but isn't in packed.

My third is in over and vacuum and five,

My fourth is in child and bright and alive.

My fifth is in good but is also in bad,

My last is in made but isn't in mad.

My whole is about learning to share things out.

Just ask your teacher what I'm all about.

111

30 Maisie was learning about adjectives. She asked her English teacher for help. 'Miss Stuart, which is correct: My brother chose the bigger half of the cake - or the biggest half of the cake?' What did Miss Stuart say?

31 There are 18 letters in the English alphabet. How can this be?

32 The average English word is five letters long, although it's easy to think of words with more than 10 letters. What is the longest word in the English language?

Answers on page 170

33 What's wrong with a story that's set on a Saturday and Sunday?

34 What Is Missing?

How quickly can you find out what is so unusual about this paragraph? It looks so ordinary that you would think that nothing is wrong with it at all, and in fact, nothing is. But it is unusual. Why? If you study it and think about it, you may find out, but I am not going to assist you in any way. You must do it without coaching. No doubt, if you work at it for long, it will dawn on you. Who knows? Go to work and test your skill!

35 The singular forms of the verb 'to be' are: 'I am,' 'you are,' and 'he, she, or it is.' However, can you think of an example where you would be correct in saying, 'I is'?

113

Riddles at School

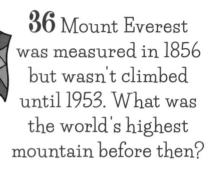

36 Mount Everest was measured in 1856 but wasn't climbed until 1953. What was the world's highest mountain before then?

37 What is the capital of Antarctica?

38 What has four eyes and a mouth, and runs but has no legs?

39 Where is the best place in the USA to learn your multiplication tables?

Answers on page 170

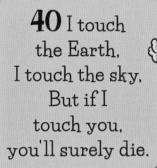

40 I touch the Earth, I touch the sky, But if I touch you, you'll surely die.

41 My feet stay warm, but my head is cold. No one can move me, I'm just too old.

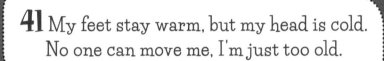

42 I rest near the shore, never touching the sea, I bring worlds together, yet people cross me.

43 From my mouth belch black clouds and red-hot rain. You could sail upon my river, but your ship would be in flame.

115

Answers on page 170

44 SPORTS QUIZ

A) Which athlete reaches the top of his or her game and is happy that it's all downhill from there?

B) In which sport do ALL the players go backward?

C) What sport uses a hard white ball and begins with a 'T'?

45 What did the baseball glove say to the baseball?

46 Mr. Jennings the PE teacher is one of the 36 percent of teachers in his school who are left-handed. However, he plays racket sports right-handed. Which hand does he use to stir his coffee?

116

Answers on page 170

47 Mr. Tozer is known for being competitive. One day, he points to himself and then to each member of his class. 'We may not be the fastest; we may never win a gold medal; we may never score the most goals. But every one of us has held a world record at some point. What is it?'

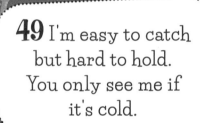

48 When the fire bell rang during Miss Smith's lesson, she didn't direct her pupils to any of the fire exits. Why not?

49 I'm easy to catch but hard to hold. You only see me if it's cold.

50 Jimmy has lost his football socks – again. And the light isn't working in the lost-and-found closet – again. There are 17 blue socks and 21 yellow socks in lost-and-found. How many socks must Jimmy grab in the darkness to make sure he gets a matching pair?

Answers on page 171

51 What does a violinist say when she gets her notes wrong?

52 What's this? Thin skin, round sound.

53 This Spanish instrument is also something that a fisherman might do. What is it?

Answers on page 171

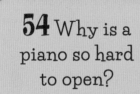

54 Why is a piano so hard to open?

55 Mystery Word

EACH LINE OF THIS PUZZLE IS A CLUE TO A DIFFERENT LETTER. CAN YOU DISCOVER THE HIDDEN WORD?

My first is in forte and twice
in quartet,
My second's in reed but not in duet.
My third is in flute and tuba and drum.
My fourth can be heard at the end
of rhythm.
My fifth is in pitch, piano, and tempo.
My sixth is in volume and twice
in crescendo.
My seventh completes me and
ends instrument;
I'm used to announce an
important event!

Answers on page 171

56 If your science teacher drops a coin into a beaker of water at 20 degrees Centigrade, and at the same time, you drop a coin into a beaker of water at 20 degrees Fahrenheit, which coin will sink faster?

57 What has a funny bone but can't laugh?

58 If a doctor is in danger of catching a cold, what is a pilot likely to catch?

Answers on page 171

59 Two of the Earth's nearest stars are Sirius and Wolf. Sirius is 8.7 light years away and moving toward Earth at 8 km/sec (5 miles/second). Wolf is 7.7 light years away but moving away from Earth at 13 km/sec (8 miles/second). After 2 light years, which will be the nearest star to the Earth?

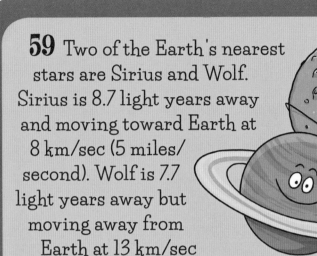

60 What grows when you feed it but dies when you give it a drink?

61 Which chemical substance is this?
H I J K L M N O

62 When is a blue textbook not a blue textbook?

121

63 Mystery Word

EACH LINE OF THIS PUZZLE IS A CLUE TO A DIFFERENT
LETTER. CAN YOU DISCOVER THE HIDDEN WORD?

My first ends pharaoh, an
Egyptian prince.
My second's in birth and also in since.
My third's in Medusa, Cyclops,
and serpent,
My fourth closes feast and banquet
and servant.
My next is in Trojan and second in horse.
My sixth is in secret, in crack, and
in Morse.
My last is the question that's
not who, where, when –
But the 'when' in this
subject is
always 'back then.'

64 Why were so
many Impressionist
painters French?

Answers on page 171

65 Some novels start at the end and go backward in time. Can you think of a famous book where August comes before July?

66 Here is a word – six letters it contains. Subtract the last and only twelve remain.

67 What appears once in a minute, twice in a moment, but never in a hundred years?

123

68 Have you heard of a Tom Swifty? It's a sentence that ends in an adverb describing the way Tom is speaking, but the same adverb also gives the sense of the whole statement. For instance, 'I should have written down all the ingredients I need to buy,' said Tom listlessly. Can you complete these examples?

'I itch all over, but I won't visit the doctor!' shouted Tom _ _ _ _ ly.

'I know how to make the light work!' explained Tom _ _ _ _ _ _ _ _ ly.

'I hate it when it's so cold,' grumbled Tom _ _ _ _ _ _ ly.

'I just knocked down all ten pins!' whooped Tom _ _ _ _ _ _ _ ly.

124

Answers on page 172

Underwater
Riddles

1 If a fisherman brings home 20 buckets of fish, and his father brings home 40 buckets, who has the most fish?

2 What never gets any wetter, no matter how hard it rains?

3 What happens when you throw a white shell into the Red Sea?

Answers on page 172

4 What am I? If you can hear where I come from, I am no longer there ...

5 What did the mermaid say to the salmon after his girlfriend left him for a shark?

6 What is found on land and at sea, although it can't be seen from either; it can be harnessed but not held, and it has no mouth, but it can be heard?

127

Answers on page 172

7 Which letter of the alphabet has the most water?

8 What kind of house weighs the least?

9 Four men were on a fishing trip. A storm blew up and capsized their boat, throwing all of them into the ocean. When they were rescued, every single man was still dry. Why is that?

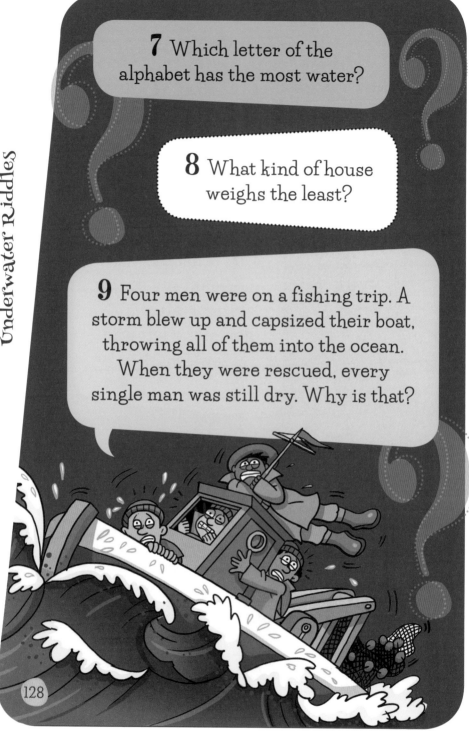

128

10 Mystery Word

EACH LINE OF THIS PUZZLE IS A CLUE TO A LETTER.
CAN YOU DISCOVER THE HIDDEN WORD?

My first is in ran but isn't in far,
My second's in sea but isn't in star.
My third is in scallop and porpoise
and pearl.
My fourth's in typhoon, in twist,
and in twirl.
My fifth's in kahuna and also outside,
My first now comes back again, just
like the tide.
My last is in water and ocean
and home.
My whole is a god from mythical Rome.

11 How is the letter 't' like
an island?

Answers on page 173

12 What phrase is written here?
CCCCCCC

13 What's the difference between an iceberg and a clothes brush?

14 A man keeps a speedboat moored in the marina. The boat's ladder hangs over the side, and at low tide, the bottom rung just touches the water. The rungs are 30 cm (1 ft) apart. How many rungs will be underwater when the tide rises by 1 m (3 ft)?

Answers on page 173

15 A ship's crew is caught in a tropical storm. They all take shelter apart from Captain Crick. He braves the elements and the lashing rain. He has no raincoat, no hat, and no umbrella. His clothes are totally soaked, rain drips from the end of his nose, and yet not a hair on his head gets wet. How can this be?

16 What is the strongest creature in the sea?

17 Which single word can be added to all these other words to make well-known phrases?
Mexican ... Micro ...
Ocean ...   Radio ...

131

18 Imagine you are deep-sea diving. You come face to face with a great white shark. You're terrified! What should you do?

19 What sea creature can swim as fast as it likes, but it never gets away from home?

20 What kind of horse do fish ride?

132

Answers on page 173

21 I have a beak but not a tail.
I swim around but am not a whale.
My legs are long, but I can't walk.
My brain is large, but I can't talk.
What am I?

22 Why are sea creatures with shells not fun to be with?

23 What runs into the ocean but stays in its bed the whole time?

133

24 Two dolphins are playing in the ocean. Dolphin A is behind dolphin B - but dolphin B is behind dolphin A. How can that be?

25 I am strong enough to walk on and heavy enough to crush roofs. But just a little sunlight will make me vanish! What am I?

26 What can be found in the middle of an ocean, that can't be found in the Atlantic or the Pacific?

Answers on page 174

27 Mystery Word

EACH LINE OF THIS PUZZLE
IS A CLUE TO A LETTER. CAN YOU DISCOVER
THE HIDDEN WORD?

My first is in cottonwood, in
cedar, and in beech,
My second's in banana and also
in peach.
My third is in launch and rowing
and motion.
My fourth is in swordfish as well as
in ocean.
My fifth is in source and also in
end,
My whole is a boat you can use
with a friend.

28 What has five eyes and
runs through the USA?

Answers on page 174

29 What happened to the pianist who worked on a cruise ship?

30 What kind of tree can you carry in your hand?

31 Two cruise ships are crossing the Atlantic Ocean. The blue ship leaves Great Britain on Tuesday. The red ship leaves the United States on Thursday but is moving twice as fast. Which ship will be closer to the USA when they pass one another?

Answers on page 174

32 A zoologist is walking through a jungle and finds something in her pocket. It has a tail and a head but no legs. How does she know it's not dangerous?

33 An explorer is paddling up a river, when he comes to a place where it splits two ways. One way leads to a city of gold ... and the other way leads to a waterfall! He has two guides with him. One guide can only tell the truth, and the other always lies. But he doesn't know which is which. What question should the explorer ask to make sure he takes the right route?

Answers on page 174

34 A man goes scuba diving and comes face to face with a tiger. Last year while diving, he met a bull. How can this be?

35 Dave doesn't dare go deep-sea diving in Dominica every year. Can you spell all that without any 'd's?

36 What is the number one use of shark skin in the world?

Answers on page 175

37 Two pirates are standing on opposite sides of a ship. One looks west and the other east – yet they can see each other clearly. How is that?

38 What comes down but never goes up?

39 Elephants have two, but I have only one; Flippers are my arms, legs I have none. Although I'm a mammal, on land I'm never found; I live where it's coldest, the whole year round. What am I?

139

Answers on page 175

40 Can you find the name of a sea creature hidden within each of these sentences? The first one has been done for you:

(A) She wanted to wear her new tuTU, NAturally.

(B) Is that tiara yours, or did you borrow it?

(C) In case of fire, don't panic or alarm the horses.

(D) He built a lavish ark in the yard for them to play on.

41 I'm the part of the bird that's not in the sky. I can surf over the ocean but always stay dry. What am I?

Answers on page 175

42 Where does a fish keep its money?

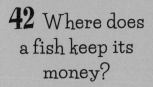

43 Mystery Word

EACH LINE OF THIS PUZZLE IS A CLUE TO A LETTER.
CAN YOU DISCOVER THE HIDDEN WORD?

My first is in swim and wetsuit
and splash,
My second's in hush but isn't
in crash.
My third is in ride but isn't
in dive.
My next is in four and also in five.
My fifth is in breaker, in tide, and
in wave.
My sixth is in fright and
also in brave.
My whole is a dude who
hangs out with a board,
Perfecting a skill that is
widely adored.

141

44 If a cruise ship sinks halfway between Australia and New Zealand, in which country would they bury the survivors?

45 What won't break if you throw it off the roof of the highest building in the world, but will fall apart if you drop it into the ocean?

46 Redbeard the pirate is boasting about his many wives. 'All of them are redheads, except two. All are blondes, except two. And all are brunettes, except two.' How many wives does he actually have?

Answers on page 175

47 When Stuart goes to beach, he does something fun. When written down, this word looks the same the right way up and upside down. He ...

48 Rough and dull as rock, I'm plain as plain can be. But hidden deep inside, there's great beauty in me. What am I?

49 How can you turn a book into a stream?

143

50 There are two penguins in front of two other penguins. There are two penguins behind two other penguins. There are two penguins in between two penguins. How many penguins are there?

51 What can build castles, break down mountains, make some blind, and help others to see?

52 What did the ocean say to the beach?

Answers on page 176

53 A word of eight letters, found on the sea floor. To help with your guesses, I'll tell you some more. My first half guides sailors back home in the dark; My second half makes a nice meal for a shark!

54 What kind of rocks are found in the Nile River?

55 What runs from front to back on one side of a ship, and from back to front on the other side?

145

56 Mystery Word

EACH LINE OF THIS PUZZLE IS A CLUE TO A LETTER. CAN
YOU DISCOVER THE HIDDEN WORD?

My first is in turtle but isn't in tortoise.
My second's in yard and also in
porpoise.
My third is in haddock and mackerel
and perch.
My fourth is in hunt and also
in search.
My fifth is in seaside and pier but isn't
in sea,
My last is in nail and also in knee.
I look like a plant, but on closer
inspection,
You'll see I'm an animal, with spines for
protection.

57 What
kind of hair do
surfers have?

146

58 Did you know that you can spell fish as 'ghoti'? Why is that?

59 Why is it easy to weigh fish?

60 Sailors throw it away when they need to use it, but they take it around with them when they're done with it. What is it?

147

Take a deep breath, then see how fast you can say these tongue-twisters!

Six slippery snailfish slid slowly seaward.

She saw a fish on the seashore, and I'm sure the fish she saw was a sawfish.

She sells seashells on the seashore.
If she sells seashells on the seashore,
Where are the shells she sells?

Fresh fried fish,
fish fresh fried,
fried fish fresh,
fish fried fresh.

Answers

Animal Riddles

Page 6
1 Swap the 'P' in polar bear and it becomes solar bear.
2 A snail. (You couldn't carry your home!)
3 A sheep.

Page 7
4 They don't – they have bear feet!
5 It has gone in a straight line 5 km (3 miles) north to the North Pole, then 3 km (2 miles) onward, now heading south.
6 Because if they lived by the bay, they'd be bagels!
7 A fish.

Page 8
8 Baby giraffes.
9 A giraffe's shadow.
10 Because they taste funny!

Page 9
11 A mole.
12 A snake.
13 Footsteps.

Page 10
14 Nine weeks. (You don't need to multiply! The number doubles every week, so a week before Tom has 1,024 mice, he will have 512 mice.)
15 It's a computer lesson, and they are computer mice.
16 A carpet!
17 Tough cheese!

Page 11

18 Because they are always spotted.
19 Warthog.

Page 12

20 He gets closer and closer, but he never reaches the edge.
21 A fox.
22 Out of bounds!

Page 13

23 The riddle says it is not to one side of him. That's because it is on the other side of him!
24 A lonfsh.
25 An egg.

Page 14

26 His horse is named Friday.
27 Lioness. Take away 'l', 'i', 's', and 's,' and 'one' is left. The lion is 'king of the beasts,' so she must be queen!.
28 'Bye, son!' (Bison - gettit?)

Page 15

29 First he takes the rat across and rows back. Then he takes the snake across, but when he rows back, he brings the rat with him. He leaves the rat again and rows over with the grain. He rows back with an empty boat, then finally takes the rat across.
30 Lots of animals can - elephants can't jump!
31 A hot dog.

Page 16

32 You don't - you get down (feathers) from a duck.
33 Humans - they crawl in early life, walk on two legs as adults, and by the end of their life, they use a walking stick to help them.
34 A dog - in the winter, it wears a coat, but in the summer, it wears a coat and pants!

Page 17

35 The other end of the string isn't tied to anything.
36 He is playing 'Snakes and Ladders.'
37 When it is a chess piece.

Page 18

38 When it is a cob (a male swan).
39 A person riding a horse.
40 A hippo.

Page 19

41 None - peacocks are male and don't lay eggs.
42 Polar bears and seals live in the Arctic - penguins do not. They live in the Antarctic.
43 Fur or hair.
44 The letter 'g.'

Page 20

45 Just one - me! When I met them, they were coming from the opposite direction, away from St. Ives.
46 A zebra.

Page 21

47 Because you take photos with a camera, not with a baby elephant.
48 Six elephants - read the riddle carefully!
49 The lion's shadow.

Page 22

50 An upside-down centipede.
51 None - monkeys cannot talk.
52 Drop it from 4 m (13 ft) in the air. It will fall the first 3 m (10 ft) without breaking!

Page 23

53 A snail.
54 Because they're shellfish!
55 He kept ducks.
56 A nail in a horseshoe.

Page 24

57 Import-ant!
58 Koala.

Page 25

59 Only one - after that, it is no longer an empty truck.
60 The letter 'a'.
61 A bat.

Page 26
62 Gorilla.
63 London ('lon' is ¾ of lion; 'don' is the first half of donkey).

Page 27
64 Only halfway; after that, it is walking out of the forest.
65 Panda.
66 A dinosaur.
67 He was bare hunting!

Around the Home

Page 30
1 Glass!
2 The carpet.
3 A key.

Page 31
4 The noise of the car's engine.
5 The letter 'r'.
6 Roller skates.
7 A garbage truck (it is surrounded by flies – the insects – because of the garbage).

Page 32
8 The doorbell or the telephone.
9 A bell.
10 Silence.
11 Matt!

Page 33
12 Bedroom.
13 Finger tips!

Page 34
14 Your name.
15 A needle.
16 He just went to the hairdresser for a haircut.

Page 35
17 A chair.
18 A nail.
19 A pack of cards.
20 An alarm clock.

Page 36
21 A pair of shoes.
22 A glove.
23 Because nothing happened when he pressed the buttons.
24 A turtleneck jumper.

Page 37
25 They bought a pair of choux buns!
26 A shoe.
27 When it's a coat of paint.
28 Clean underwear.

Page 38
29 'Short.'
30 A pillow ('pill' + 'ow').
31 A coin.
32 Rosie.

Page 39

33 Garage.

34 Neither – candles burn shorter.

Page 40

35 She threw the ball straight up in the air.

36 A tennis ball (as well as a volleyball and a shuttlecock).

37 Pawns in a chess game.

Page 41

38 Teeth.

39 A colander or sieve.

40 A pin and a needle.

Page 42

41 They are two sons out of triplets (or more).

42 The more you have, the longer you'll live!

43 A clock.

44 Noon.

Page 43

45 A clock and a sundial. They both tell the time, but the sundial does not work at night.

46 Envelope.

47 A stamp.

48 All of them! And some have even more...

Page 44

49 Clockwise. It doesn't matter which hand you use, but it does matter whether you're turning the bulb or the socket.

50 A map.

51 Flying saucers.

52 Chili sauce.

Page 45

53 A mirror.

54 A towel.

55 A sponge.

56 Scales.

Page 46

57 They have their backs to each other.

58 Give an apple to your mother and one to your dad, hand one to your brother... and give the bag with the last apple in it to your sister.

59 On a clock: 11:00 plus 2 hours is 1:00.

Page 47

60 When Jack sits down, Jill runs around the chair twice, and then says, 'I'll come back tomorrow to run around it a third time!'

61 A balloon or a bubble.

Page 48

62 He is buying house numbers to fix on the door.
63 A joke.
64 Scissors.

Page 49

65 A computer keyboard.
66 The living room!
67 A battery.
68 A book.

Page 50

69 Toaster.
70 When it's ajar!

Page 51

71 They're the hands on a clock.
72 Arm, leg, eye, ear, lip, hip,
gum, jaw, rib, toe.

Down on the Farm

Page 54

1 True - there are only two capital 'F's;
the others are lower case 'f'.

2 A field of corn.

3 None. Acorns grow on oak trees,
not chestnut trees.

Page 55

4 Neither - the yolk is yellow!

5 Seven. He sold four eggs to the first customer (half
of seven is 3½ plus the other half = 4 eggs), two to the
second person (half of the remaining three eggs = 1½, plus
the other half = 2 eggs), and one to the third (half of the
remaining egg, plus the other half = 1).

6 When they are going cheap!

Page 56

7 A hole.

8 A tree (a deciduous
tree, that is!).

9 10.

Page 57

10 Cattle.

11 In a sty-scraper!

159

Page 58

12 Two cows in a field.
13 The Moon.
14 One!

Page 59

15 Farmer Jennings was walking through town.
16 When it's a greyhound.
17 A veteran.

Page 60

18 Thunderbolt: 'th' under 'bolt'.
19 An icicle.
20 The wind

Page 61

21 Snow.
22 A rainbow.
23 Daisy is a cow and sleeps in a field.

Page 62

24 Eyes.
25 A splinter.
26 Pants.

Page 63

27 Saddle.
28 14. It's '20 SICK sheep', but your friend will hear '26'.

Page 64

29 The truck would have burned off more than 30 grams (1 ounce) of fuel in the first 1.6 km (1 mile) of crossing the bridge. Therefore the sparrow's weight would have no effect.
30 He tractor down!
31 Ducks or geese.

Page 65
32 The letter 'd'.
33 A ton. Written backward, it spells 'not'!
34 Normal – it's best to have half your fingers on each hand.

Page 66
35 The match.
36 Swallow.
37 'That's a re-leaf'.

Page 67
38 Just one to complete it.
39 A farmer on horseback chewing an ear of corn.
40 A river.

Page 68
41 The river is frozen.
42 A horse.
43 The temperature.

Page 69
44 Potato.
45 When it turns into a field.

Page 70
46 None – the bang of the gun will frighten away the others.
47 A windmill.
48 He thought he might get a kick out of it.

161

Page 71

49 Darkness.
50 Only four. The cat and dog have paws, and the cows have hooves.
51 Laughing stock.

Page 72

52 Five - she sold half (2.5) plus a half (2.5 + 0.5 = 3), so she started with 3 + 2.
53 A chick in an egg (or a butterfly in a chrysalis).
54 Bark!

Page 73

55 O I C U!
56 An udder failure.
57 A seahorse.
58 Jack, with a clean face, saw Billy's face and figured that his must be dirty, too - so his mother would know what he'd been up to. Billy could only see Jack's clean face, so he would assume that his face was also clean.

Page 74

59 His hood or his umbrella.
60 Donkey.

Page 75

61 37 days. At the end of day one, the worm would be at the 2.5-cm (1-inch) mark. At the end of the 35th day, the worm would be at the 89-cm (35-inch) mark. On the 36th day, the worm travels from 89 cm (35 inches) to 99 cm (39 inches), but it slips back to 91 cm (36 inches). On the 37th day, the worm climbs 10 cm (4 inches), which is enough for it to climb out of the hole.

62 Day breaks and night falls.

63 Fooling with a bee!

64 Neither side - roosters don't lay eggs!

Mealtime Mysteries

Page 78

1 Yes - it's highly unlikely that an unboiled egg will crack a concrete floor.

2 Breakfast and dinner.

3 Pea.

Page 79

4 A chili dog is hotter (spicier) than a hot dog.

5 A cherry.

6 There is one 'p' in 'a pod'.

Page 80
7 Nacho cheese ('not your cheese')!
8 Lettuce. Just listen as you say it!
9 Edam (read it backward ...).

Page 81
10 Pickle.
11 An orange.
12 They're not into fast food.

Page 82
13 Teapot.
14 Water. Cows make milk, but they don't drink it!
15 A hiccup.
16 A bottle.

Page 83
17 The letter 'i'.
18 Bread.
19 A doughnut.

Page 84
20 A brown 'e'.
21 Eight carrots.
22 An apple.

Page 85
23 Eat, heat, wheat.
24 An egg.
25 A pineapple.

Page 86

26 Cabbage.
27 Potatoes (pot + 8 Os).
28 Grapes.
29 Just five. Imagine that you start with 20 oranges each. You'll end up with 15, and your friend will have 25.

Page 87

30 Spinach.
31 A flip-flop!
32 Potato (take away 'ato' and you're left with 'pot').

Page 88

33 Your mother – you are only carrying bags, not groceries.
34 Popcorn.
35 A watermelon.

Page 89

36 A mushroom.
37 The apple – it is the only one that can be eaten without removing its outer layer.
38 Four minutes. The arithmetic part was to confuse you.

Page 90

39 There are only three people: grandfather, father, and son (the grandfather is also father to the father).

40 A potato.

Page 91

41 Ice cream.

42 He is wearing his uniform.

43 Corn on the cob.

44 The charcoal in a barbecue.

Page 92

45 2.05. (And the sauce costs 0.05, which is 2.00 less).

46 A coconut tree.

47 10. Friends will not feel full of food after eating if they feel that your food is merely a trifle!

Page 93

48 Deli foods.

49 Egg.

50 Lemon and melon.

Page 94

51 Because there are a lot more Chinese people.

52 C and y.

53 An onion.

54 Fruit flies like eating fruit. (Fruit flies are small insects!)

Page 95
55 Six (two of each flavor).
56 Pepper.

Page 96
57 Turn off the running water.
58 Pick up the second glass and pour the water into the fifth glass.

Page 97
59 A hole.
60 An avocado.
61 Above Marie's head.

Page 98
62 Walnut.
63 Lettuce.
64 Two - because you took away two!

Page 99
65 Stone.
66 Wheat or bread.
67 Very large hands!

Riddles at School

Page 102

1 She asked if he was asleep and he said, 'Yes!'
2 There are twelve 'seconds' in a year: January 2nd, February 2nd, March 2nd, and so on ...
3 Read it out loud: Too wise you are, too wise you be, I see you are too wise for me!

Page 103

4 Well, they may be lazy or rude, or they may have figured out that there's no way to hide something between pages 57 and 58 of a book, since they are the two sides of the same piece of paper.
5 AD 6. There is no year 0, so when you count, you jump from 1 BC to AD 1.
6 Postbox.

Page 104

7 The smallest possible number is three: girl - boy - boy.
8 11 - Boys often play football at school, and girls often choose to play hockey.
9 The word 'wholesome'.

Page 105

10 Sentence.
11 The elfabet.

Page 106

12 A bubble has an inside and an outside.

13 You will always get the answer 'four'. No matter how many times you attempt it, $2 \times 2 = 4$.

14 The first number was zero, which means it doesn't matter what other numbers are given, the answer will always be zero.

Page 107

15 $888 + 88 + 8 + 8 + 8 = 1,000$

16 Forty.

17 Homework.

Page 108

18 The one dated AD 798, since the other must be a fake. No one in the year 368 BC could have predicted the dating system we use (they wouldn't know how many years BC it was!).

19 Because he was still alive.

20 None – they were babies when they were born.

Page 109

21 Friendship.

22 A sword, because 'the pen is mightier than the sword'.

23 An arrow.

24 A castle.

Page 110

25 A somersault: summer + salt.

26 A pencil.

27 A clock.

Page 111

28 $4 + 5 = 9$.

29 Divide.

Page 112

30 Neither is right – two halves of a cake are equal in size.

31 There are 18 letters in the phrase 'the English alphabet'.

32 'Language' is the longest word in 'the English language'.

Page 113

33 It has a weak end.

34 The whole text does not contain the letter 'e', even though it is one of the most commonly used letters in the English language.

35 'I' is the ninth letter of the alphabet,' or 'I' is one of the five vowels.

Page 114

36 It was still Mount Everest – measuring or climbing it didn't change its height.

37 The letter 'A'.

38 The Mississippi River.

39 Times Square.

Page 115

40 Lightning.

41 A mountain.

42 A bridge.

43 A volcano.

Page 116

44 A) A skier.

B) Tug of war. (In rowing, one person sits facing forward).

C) Golf. It begins with a tee!

45 'Catch you later!'

46 He really ought to use a spoon.

Page 117

47 Being the youngest person in the whole world.
48 They were doing PE outdoors on the playing field.
49 Your breath.
50 Three socks – at least two of them will be the same.

Page 118

51 'Fiddlesticks!'
52 A drum.
53 Castanet.

Page 119

54 Because the keys are on the inside.
55 Trumpet.

Page 120

56 The coin in the first beaker. 20 degrees Fahrenheit is below freezing, so the water in the beaker will be frozen solid.
57 A skeleton.
58 A plane.

Page 121

59 The Sun.
60 Fire.
61 Water – H_2O.
62 When it is red (or 'read')!

Page 122

63 History.
64 Because they were born in France.

Page 123
65 The dictionary!
66 Dozens.
67 The letter 'm'.

Page 124
68 Rashly; brightly (or perhaps brilliantly); bitterly (or you could use icily); strikingly.

Underwater Riddles

Page 126
1 The fisherman - if his father's buckets are empty.
2 The ocean.
3 It makes a splash. (Of course, it doesn't turn pink! Don't be silly ...)

Page 127
4 A seashell. If you can hear the sound of the ocean by holding it to your ear, the shell is no longer in the ocean.
5 Don't worry - there are plenty more fish in the sea.
6 The wind.

Page 128

7 The 'c'.
8 A lighthouse.
9 All four men were married – so no 'single' men were there to get wet!

Page 129

10 Neptune.
11 It's in the middle of water.

Page 130

12 The seven seas.
13 One crushes boats, and the other brushes coats!
14 None – the boat and the ladder will rise with the tide.

Page 131

15 He is bald.
16 A mussel.
17 Wave.

Page 132

18 Stop imagining!
19 A turtle.
20 A seahorse.

Page 133

21 An octopus.
22 They are so crabby!
23 A river.

Page 134

24 They have their backs to each other.
25 Ice.
26 The letter 'e'.

Page 135

27 Canoe.
28 The Mississippi River.

Page 136

29 She got middle-C-sickness.
30 A palm tree.
31 When the two ships meet, they will both be exactly the same distance from the United States.

Page 137

32 It's a coin she put there yesterday.
33 He should ask one guide, 'Which way would the other guide tell me to go?' - and then take the opposite route. Here's why: the guide who tells the truth will honestly tell the explorer that the liar will tell him the wrong way. The guide who lies will tell the explorer a fib about the honest man's answer. Either way, the explorer needs to do the opposite of what he is told.

Page 138

34 They are both types of shark.
35 Yes - 'all that'!
36 Covering sharks, of course!

Page 139

37 The pirates are facing inward, not outward.
38 Rain, hail, or snow.
39 A narwhal (which has a single tusk instead of two, like an elephant).

Page 140

40 RAY: Is that tiara yours, or did you borrow it?
 CORAL: In case of fire, don't panic or alarm the horses.
 SHARK: He built a lavish ark in the yard for them to play on.
41 The bird's shadow.

Page 141

42 In the riverbank!
43 Surfer.

Page 142

44 Neither - you don't bury survivors!
45 A tissue.
46 Three - one redhead, one blonde, and one brunette.

Page 143

47 SWIMS

48 An oyster with a pearl inside.

49 Add the letter 'r' to make 'brook'.

Page 144

50 Four.

51 Sand. You can make sand castles on the beach; sand carried by wind or waves can erode a mountain over time; you won't be able to see if you get sand in your eyes; glass is made out of sand.

52 Nothing - it just waved!

Page 145

53 Starfish.

54 Wet ones.

55 The ship's name.

Page 146

56 Urchin.

57 Wavy!

Page 147

58 The 'gh' is pronounced as in the word 'rough'; the 'o' as in 'women', and the 'ti' as in 'station'.

59 Because they have their own scales.

60 An anchor.